Glen Is Glad

By Clem King

Glen was glum.

It was wet, and it was not fun!

"Let's see all the things you are glad of!" said Mum.

"Like what?" said Glen.

"You have lots of big shells!" said Mum.

"Yes, I am glad of my shells," said Glen.

"You can sing well!"
said Mum.

"Yes! I sang in the Glam Cup,"
said Glen.

"I am glad to have
Gloss the fish!" said Glen.

"Gloss is glad to get fed!"
said Mum.

"And I am glad I can kick well," said Glen.

"But not in here, Glen!" said Mum.

Glug, glug, glug!

CHECKING FOR MEANING

1. Why was Glen glum? *(Literal)*

2. What was Glen glad of? *(Literal)*

3. Why didn't Mum want Glen to kick the ball inside? *(Inferential)*

EXTENDING VOCABULARY

glum	What does it mean to be *glum*? What might make you feel glum? What are other words that have a similar meaning?
glad	How do you feel if you are *glad*? Are you happy or sad? Can you think of another word with a similar meaning? E.g. pleased.
glug	*Glug* describes the sound of Glen drinking choc milk. What do we call this type of word? I.e. onomatopoeia. What other word could the author have used?

MOVING BEYOND THE TEXT

1. When have you felt glum? What made you feel that way?

2. What makes you feel glad?

3. What do you do inside when it is too wet to play outside?

4. What is something you really like to eat or drink?

SPEED SOUNDS

| bl | gl | cr | fr | st |

PRACTICE WORDS

Glen

glum

glad

Glam

Gloss

glug